THE KNOPF POETRY SERIES

also by Alan Williamson

*Pity the Monsters: The Political Vision
of Robert Lowell*

PRESENCE

Alan Williamson

PRESENCE

POEMS

Alfred A. Knopf   New York   1983

THIS IS A BORZOI BOOK
PUBLISHED BY ALFRED A. KNOPF, INC.

The poems in this book originally appeared in the following: "Arrangements"
(the third part of "Trois Gymnopédies"), "C., Again," "Last Autumn in Charlottes-
ville," and "Spring Trains" in *The New Yorker*. "Aubade, Reconstructed in Tran-
quility," "Childless Couple," "Customs of the Barbarians," "The First Spring
Nights," and "Old Toys Come Back" in *Poetry*. "If, on Your First Love's Wedding
Day" in *Poetry Northwest*. Other selections appeared in the following publications:
Massachusetts Review, *The New Review*, *Padan Aram*, *The Paris Review*, *Partisan
Review*, *Ploughshares*, *Shenandoah*, *Skyline*, *The Virginia Quarterly Review*, and
The Yale Review; and in the anthologies *Ten American Poets* (Carcanet Press,
1973) and *Landscape and Distance: Contemporary Poets from Virginia* (University
Press of Virginia, 1975).

The writing of these poems was facilitated by the generosity of several organizations.
I would like to thank the National Endowment for the Arts for a fellowship grant
in 1973–74; the University of Virginia for a Sesquicentennial Associateship in 1974;
The Artists Foundation (Massachusetts) for a fellowship in 1980; and the Michael
Karolyi Memorial Foundation for my stay there in the fall of 1976.

Library of Congress Cataloging in Publication Data
Williamson, Alan. [date] Presence.
(Knopf poetry series; #9)
I. Title.
PS3573.I45623P7   813'.54   82–47964
ISBN 0–394–52850–6   AACR2
ISBN 0–394–71259–5 (pbk.)

Manufactured in the United States of America
First Edition

For Anne

Contents

I

Friends Who Have Failed

They leave from positions of strength, like all baroque
civilizations; leave the statues we cannot imagine moving
for heaviness caught in the skirts . . .
We watch their gestures grow finer and more nervous
in the widening air.
They are the best judges of wine; talk always at the glittering edges
of things, the terrible auras . . . The afternoons in their houses
hang upside down, like objects seen through wine.
Their footfalls die an inch away in the carpet.

And leaving, we wonder why the world
has not appreciated this fineness; why clumsier juggling
finds favor in its slow eye . . .
But we have not understood the world; how its way
is to destroy without destroying, the way air
levels a mountain; things fly apart in a vacuum . . .
It wears us to the hard thing we cannot help being;
and if the only hard thing is our determination
not to be hard, it wears us down to that.

Leaving for Islands

Ormos Athinios, Thira

Morning comes, and the baked look
of rising early on people's faces;
or evening, and the cool with a trace of rot in it
lifts off the face of the waves.

And in the concrete café, the simple blank
shoulders of fascination, changed in no year;
with emptiness in their mouths—for *we live
the death, we die the life, of the gods.*

Cycladic driftstones!—smoothed as the deepest
shapes in the mind; or islands
we expect beyond islands, each more
treeless and roadless, a coagulant

clangor of bronze on water,
like the sky's sperm when Aphrodite rose . . .
And I wonder if anyone is ever young
or ruthless enough, to live there

entirely. Dolphins won't take us. We must wait
till the ship that carries the city's
inner crush of black olive, shit, black tar
to its shakiest rivet—hours late—stands tiny

inside the dead crater. And now a few
slowly shoulder their backpacks; and now one
girl is dumbly attentive, while a boy plucks thin
songs of his—our—homeland.

August 1977

4

For Robinson Jeffers

More and more I think about you, and the others—
your likes and unlikes—who chose to harden their difference
until it was so dense, it would shine of itself in the dark;
lived narrow into towers, to the faces of wives and children
loved more steadily than most; turned their even-planed desks
    to the ocean;
and built the beds they would die in into the stonework
of their hand-made houses, trying to care as little
for fame as the dead, or hawks . . .

                    Oh, I know
all one might say: that what you fled and resented
was the father within; or, worse, some incapacity
you half-knew in yourself, and could not cure;
that the more your peace was accomplished, the harder a spectral
humanity seethed from behind the planted forest,
from the cities as you dreamed them . . . till the love of yourself
    you began with
half-recoiled at the self it had made . . .

And yet . . . to become something simply
because one can imagine it, and it isn't there;
to say—as I half-hear you—*the others have chosen*
to elaborate the surface, until it seems to them they
are surface merely—a celluloid barely tingeing
the blank face of the streets; or else they name themselves
stones and roots, without eyes. What have they left us
even to wish for? And then, returning: those
who hated me did so not for my faults, but because
I wished to walk out of myself in a soul and a body.

House-Moving from Tournon to Besançon

Stéphane Mallarmé; Fall 1866–Spring 1867

for Bradford Cook

It's an awesome thing, when fate takes you at your word
at eighteen or twenty. *If Dreams weren't greater than Action . . .*
Happiness on this earth! One has to be pretty vulgar
to stoop to it. When I wrote that, two months
before marriage, Marie's weak chest
seemed a kind of grace-note—the blood-hearted snowdrop—
sharpening the wild-thing poignance of her eyes . . .
And *un*happiness? A curtain-line, a fling of the sleeve.
Not, at any rate, this matter of two fatigues
grinding each other; the worry when the child
gives her slight cough; the bone-cold rooms,
and happy, sometimes, for those . . .

                              Our move here was as moving
is—one's old chair in the fall rain an hour
because the men want coffee . . . The irksome part was the need
to be composed through it all; the need, after Tournon,
to think about stopping rumors before they start.

(I must tell you they fired me in mid-term. Wads,
with spit in the middle; and their parents complained of *me*.
Shoving my face forward into that brute
heaving, making it say *he loves*—
like teaching an atom to be a molecule . . .)

The moral: prompt visits
in order of rank; sincere show of interest; cards.

The town? It could hardly be less designed to lighten
such burdens: another of these ancient centers
of war and religion; drip unabsorbable; gargoyles——
The worst, though, is always God: the blank stone staring
west into nothing but its justice, as if
He were as stunned as we to have awakened . . .

Empty nets of matter; that thought our surface-glitter
was something . . .

* * *

How eagerly I waited, that first week, for life—
my only real one—to compose itself
with the room as I have it: midnight; the mirror; the window
bulged with my Dreams like firelight—like the bottomless
drawer of an old chest . . . But when I sat there, feeling
the words reach to name, then deaden on the page's
familiar virgin emptiness—the thoughts
that returned on me! Ah, my friend,
if, after these gods and ages, the realization
of all our thinking is to think itself Nothing,
why not be the truth?
                    I grew unable to feel
myself there except as a kind of skin on the thinness
of the always singular instant. Can it hide itself
in the folds of the curtain, will it run to join childhood
in the mirror-waters? I tore the drawers, for a trace
of it, of *me* . . . And the things stayed, in absolute presence,
inviting me to complete their thought with a stroke
swift, unrevisable, perfect . . .
                    I floated downward
in the un-being I glimpsed there (I can't
put this plainer—but, even in class, I lost the meaning

of the commonest words); yet half-wished it now, desiring
that every Dream should die, and—stiff and white,
as at dawn, as from the waters of that old story—the poem
of the world float free.

                              One day—gray and almost spring—
I looked in my Venetian mirror and saw the person
I had forgotten. When I say I still
need to see him there, to edge
to the next word, or thought—you will know how far I became
Nothing; or simply a gift the impersonal universe
has for thinking its causeless Idea,
our Work, the great equation
that cancels at last.
                      I have seen the ends of more than
one life; and have hardly the strength to lift my hand.

                            *   *   *

More negotiating with fools, not to spend another winter
in this terrible place. They have denied me
the Département of Lozère, unaware that my work denies them
Paradise.
                 I must say the two seem much
the same to me now, watching the first green shiver
along our pollarded plane-trees. I remember how the heat
exerted itself on things . . . A half-witted shepherd
was on trial for rape. The mind moved, behind blinds,
with the sure drift of a sleepwalker: hearing my Faun
hesitantly raise one note to the next, then flow—
and off the fountain-glitter came the nymphs
of living space and air . . .
                       I felt myself twang half-
inside things: even the hard-cased scorpions that made me
keep the bed legs sitting in cans of live gasoline.

And if one thinks the world, in that reverberation,
as if Spirit were making it, what difference?
I am trying to learn
to think that way again; not just on the squeaky
first string of the brain. On Easter, I got a terrible headache
from brain-work alone. By an enormous effort
I braced my whole chest-box, seized the impression, and rang
it inward and downward. Ever since then, when I truly
create, I am gone except for my hand and a heart
enormously hollowed and beating . . .
                              And nothing

is named now: the object
goes by in the miracle of a vibratory
near-disappearance . . .
                         into what—air, God? Who will ever know?

I need rest after all this; more rest, perhaps,
than kings are ever given. But you are not to worry;
I can't tell you the weight of peace it adds, to have taken
the future up in one's hands. I see
one book, or two, the years fallen into their crystal.
I can't think anything will have been much amiss,
if God send my old age a pleasant actress
willing to have visits in the long late afternoons.
I won't even mind much, if both her windows
and mine look out onto long railroad yards.

A Career: Matisse

There was never a time when he did not know how to paint water,
glass, and their echoes:
and as if to put the world inside, he collected
the Art Nouveau lines, the colors only the purely
superficial, child and couturier, ever saw;
until he reached the velvet bedroom of his thought,
the luxury of matter in a sweet confusion of space.

And then the fishbowl comes from the child's Euclid,
and neither feeds nor imprisons its golden flash,
the penetration of angels! Until you notice
the chair-arm overarching like Niagara . . .
then the world tears itself back and forth from the eye
like a wrap in a burlesque show.

　　　　　　　　　　And, glimpsing the sexual comedy
in this, the painter starts doing it in the round:
nudes with blank faces, nudes with arms lost in walls,
with hips and elbows blown up like hysterics' . . .
For all shape is dream, but dimension goes someplace different,
the point of fright where the known loses to the real.
You can make your Moorish girl loom through the whole blue Casbah
if you imagine, thus, her squatting; but her bedroom
slipper's lining will still shine softly redder, and farther,
the shift of a star . . .

So where does he come to it, the peace in the body
we must believe of French painters in old age?
He makes cutout dolls of women, and his woman
pastes them. His art would be an easy armchair.
It was all an old man's talk with his old whore:
he lied and lied; she was eased, and gave truth.

Van Gogh's Asylum

Here, the whitest roses
Learn the lesson that life is fire: the secret glassblower
Distends their petals, bids the small veins run
Red miles.
In the calm upland air, the cypresses
Bend with the tensile
Throat-muscles of swans.

A place to go mad or sane: as, moving
Before the self-portrait in the Jeu de Paume,
One sees the centering eye
Break into its different focus,
A swirl of paint, the green blindness
Of fish muscle in unlighted sea.

A place with a calm goodbye
For the sufferer: lines framed from the ledger,
Monsieur van Gogh est sorti guéri.

I feel the blunt legs
Of his bed reach down into the spinning,
The walls of his nights tighten
And press like a seed-pod to morning,
To days and the works thereof,

The works: the eye's never quite motiveless
Gift to the things of its death,
A breath taking in
And letting go

What is taken and goes, those stars
Shedding light in glass panes,
Cured, gone out,
Starting to die—

That earth flaring up, sun getting a chill—

Hello, goodbye.

II

A Prologue

When the nights creak open and the first musk rises
from river, reservoir, and empty brickyard,
I cannot believe he does not still come from the brightness
graphing him into his bedspread, his raveled lines,
down through the tightening streets, feeling himself thin
almost to an edge as he passes the Pilgrim
gravestones still holding their inch of haunted marshland:

to the bars hung in the night like a star-emerald.

Why shouldn't he come? To himself, he was half a vision
(then everyone younger had a lover),
and, all a vision now, he gets no further:
they surround him, the flash of eyes and throats and voices;
and if he speaks at all, it is to the homeliest,
nursing a lonely beer.

                    What is it that has short-circuited
his desire with the clear gin, the blue light on the
         mannequin's shoulder,
with the third rail in the blind subway, and the light turning
on the crushed motorcycles, the blood lost on so much tar . . .

so that he cannot believe such nights return
to common flesh, flesh like his own, and not
to the flesh of dream: fast silver metals
and the dark water, with the lights all far inside . . .

Around him, with pale rinsed hair: witches and desert planets;
they move, and he cannot move toward them: like the sun.

Dream Without End

to the memory of Joel Sunderman

Was sie mir wollen? leise soll ich des Unrechts
Anschein abtun, der ihrer Geister
reine Bewegung manchmal ein wenig behindert.

RILKE

I

I have dreamed it again, the day that you come back,
Bruce, Dick, Charlie, all of us gathered somewhere in Ohio,
Bolt upright all night in a hotel room furnished only
With a square walnut table, then filing downstairs at dawn
As your Rolls Royce pulls up like an exiled Ukrainian Count's,
    a hand
Sticks out, a Pope's, with rings; then . . . Joel, death has been
    good to you,
You're so fat you can't stand, and wrinkles cover your eyes.

II

Walking the East Village streets in hungry cold
While our filmmaker host went to Hasidic heaven on grass,
Came back to say World's End Two Years Away
(Two years whose end you didn't see),

A week before you fled
The Good Doctor, your German father, to Berlin,
We tried to thrash it out . . . your hard-won Marxism
("Nobody should have to be a hat-check girl")

Against my lapsed-Christian martyrology—
Henry James heroines, and mad John Clare,
And how Shelley outlived his death by writing it . . .
In sympathy in fear,
We talked through the night from our pallets,
Hearing in time to our voices
The plumbing cough, and down
The numbing distance of our legs
The seconds, clicking, dive . . .

And then walked out next morning into air unwarmed
By the sun though it turned the skyscrapers to mica,
And saw a child set out before us
Thrusting his shadow before him like a sword,
Trailing, then dropping a mitten . . .
A spiffy career girl in a steel-gray coat
Swerved in mid-stride
To run and return it, patting the ear-muffed head.
"They say New York is such a cold place," you said;
"But I see things like this happen all the time."

Next day,
We passed her in the same block at the same second.
She looked through us like glass.
But when I glanced over you were glancing back,
And we stomped into Bickford's, clapping our iceblock hands.

III

I remember other girls, soundlessly laughing
On the highest platforms of the fire escapes
In pullovers, combing
Their tin-blonde hair to a jet stream . . .

Then Haverford,
Our homecoming:·
Cake-white in the same cold snap, our professor's house riding
The frosting like a microcosmic toy,
With the healthy groan of the hearth-fires, and thick sleeping-
Bags tossed for us on the sleeping-porch . . .

                                   But Bobby,
Hurt by improvisations on his poetry,
Asked me why it was I kept away from women,
And was I really queer?
                        His wooden face kept coming
In pain, between
The sips of Isabel's protective vodka . . .

Then dared me to prove my manhood at a party.
Streets swam, undertowed with drink and rage.
I paced myself through wrought-up stories
About gay actor friends . . . brashly kissed
An old friend's fiancée good-night
(Acts that reversed themselves, popped "queer" or "straight"
Into my brain like colors in roulette)
Until my feet, somewhere, were shuffled
To cool wind, at the center.

Between the dorms and the house was a thin neck
Of woodland. Summer or winter,
Pissing into the blackest shrubs, or running
All the cold clearings while one breath turned to frost,
It frightened: the place of trial
Between private pain and the created home.

That night, we assayed it together.
Arms locked to shoulders, we inched down the hand-
Rail of the iced, log stairs,
Melted in mud, refrozen at crazy angles

Above the fast night road.
I pulled you down like an anchor; we broke, spun wide.
I could feel the road-ice lifting me like a tide
To the gold tangles of sleep,
The light-bulb moon
Ending the long corridors in my repeated dream
Of helpless sleeplessness . . .

                         The car
That came after to check on our safety nearly hit us.

I would thank, now, their skidding kindness; and thank Alfred,
My host, who came quietly in and unlaced my shoes
When I had laid me in full suit
Out cold, on his cold porch;
And, before all, thank Joel

Who said, next day, to Bobby,
"You could have said all that just as well of me,"
And was told, "That's obvious; but I'd never want to."

This, after I brought you "home";
My feeling, not yours, that it was kinder, saner
For you to come say goodbye.

IV

Our exhausted goodbye in 30th Street Station:
Our tossed-down, splay valises
Braced back the rush hour like spokes of a wheel
While I made my childish last demand
That you steal pages from the filmmaker's "Memoir"
Retelling (comically) my love
For a girl he wasn't able to make, either.
We both pretended

Your silent bob meant a sincere "yes,"
Because the train started to move . . .
You clutched the black briefcase to your breast and leapt,
As if you died, for my eyes, in that second . . .

In dreams, you let me know I can still write you
And it is only at the mailbox, trying to write down a Zip Code,
That I suddenly break into tears.

V

You too, like Shelley, wrote your death,
In the class yearbook, of the class suicide: "Sophomores,
We learned that we could ride the Paoli Local,
Or let it ride us."
We thought you merely callous,
Though you had shown us your father's music room, the carved
Rococo *memento moris*
In Latin, German, Portuguese, and Bunyan—
Under which star
He ruled his string quartets of fled Ukrainians
And bullied your mother straining at the keyboard.

* * *

Your whole life a child's bad Sunday,
In which you sought
The elation of crowds, rare stamps, an elegant style
As the child turns to dominoes and parcheesi . . .

And even these slow friends failed you:
Burning your frail novels
As hostages into the darkness of his will,

The last coin sold at a song
For passage to Lenin, West Berlin, willed silence . . .
"He has to have sold it," your father
Said: "There was no other way."

Gog-eyed with glasses, joints wound up like clocks,
A tiny bow at every second word . . .
Yet had to fall for the fastest girls, and sorrow
At the Piero face on the centerfold of *Playboy*;
After three failures,
You took to asking Alfred's young daughter
To prowl, with you, your fabulous antique bookstores.

Did the spiffy girl turn and start running
Down those unearthly, now, two years
(The light-years going from her eyes like glass)
To leave you something simple as a mitten
And life, set right, in your hands?

You went loveless, but came back
(Because we failed you?) love
Given over
To Caesar and slain.
You ended, for us, the unproductive pain
Of youth;
We were all the profiteers of your death.

VI

We grow by drawing inward. In our
Successes, you are wasted: Alfred's daughter with Dick; these poems
Cut from your life, but truer to you than your own.

As you, too, turned from us—"some residual fascist
Instinct for final solutions"—the one Berlin letter . . .

But it was *No Season For Tears*, when Isabel's
Eyes sparkled against the plush funeral, the family
Circling inward, the mother's ghost-spoken eulogy
Misquoting that, your best and cruelest story.
"At least there were ten of us there who really loved him!"—
Words in which we seemed to walk forth, beyond falsification.

For two years, I could imagine no other end—
Into the lanes, the night-lights' tiara, the quincunx
Of the witches' wood . . . the great house itself melting
In its mirror-gleams, back to trees . . .
                            Under a bough
We pause a moment; you ask me if I learned more
By staying to the end; and are, as you once were, patient
For my life; for my answer, as it once was, fervent
And undecided . . .
                    this year, missing in dreams,
A shape gone, and a darkness listening.

C., Again

I (BRYN MAWR, 1961)

When your feet went always naked,
tap-tapping to the Fifties rock,

it was cars leaving
for darkest America, the muscle roads, the beaches

arriving in strange wind. It froze me to your armchair,
tragic . . . and turned you elfin-angry, asking

me if, in my novel, you slept with your home-town boyfriend?
and what should one think of Castro?

You had a divorced grandmother, her drunk cousin slept too near
    the fire;
a dead mother in love

with Thomas Wolfe, and you liked blond boys with angry cars.
A brass cross from Provincetown, set among fan shells . . .

When your eyes widened, what spring.
Nothing will show me again its wild-skied, uncertain

lift in early March: your ordinary perfume,
the hills sinuous on our walks, the sound of rivulets

ending nowhere and nowhere, reaching the sea in the ear;
the sweet, sudden graveyard where I bragged of atheism . . .

Our day is ending; we go out to the diner,
old bus chrome,

the only place you let me buy you dinner.
I call myself desperate; lift hands toward your cold-kindly face,

in the green, in the neon, the haze of too much looking,
the pure oval of an old photo:

if I could leap through, I'd be father of Protestant armies . . .
How many days to divorce?

II (CHARLOTTESVILLE, 1970)

Since I have been here I have wanted
to write a poem for the football couples,
too late for the game, too early for seduction,
haunting the fields, or, when it's gray, the supermarkets
where my wife and I splurge on wines . . . Here, many
are tweedy and bloodshot already; but once, a girl
pirouettes, then stops, frightened at the reflections:
the linoleum, me, the wood wine-arbor, the window
to the heaven of ice creams . . .

O beautiful house of the dusk, and the potted meats stacked like choirs!

A weekend was something you would only go to
with boys who didn't care;
so I'm moved to know that these, too, play at couples,
as we in our shabby Penn Fruit, and pause, hushed,
as I did once, late, at the over-huge windows dim-lit
and the cash registers lonely as priests.

Two boys catch each other down telescoped aisles, and razz.

You laughed like that, like a boy.
You wore a false ring; you piled our basket with everything
that was young and useless, cake-candles, love-comics,
and were not sold. How could I have understood?
I wanted Rimbaud, the day on fire, the iron
streets smashed like glass in the dawn of our first touch.

If, on Your First Love's Wedding Day

If, on your first love's wedding day, your roommate's
locked up with the phone (which you need) and his girl
while his ex-girl sleeps on the living room sofa, homeless;
at nine, Miss Now departs; Miss Then at ten
ascends to the first-best bed; you wait in outrage
muttering Hart Crane; then she walks through your room in her slip
and doesn't see you enough to know she's teasing . . .
what do you do? Untangle the phone from the bedclothes,
and dial, your right hand sloshing gin "Here's t'Clara"

And if, when you're back, alone, calling all friends,
it's Miss Ex who drives you to the liquor store;
when the clerk doesn't know you, won't take your I.D.,
she flares up on your side, "Why, he's almost a professor!"
You come back, top down, high on gratitude,
while horse-chestnuts cast their red-prickled flowers before you
on the hood, your hair, as once with Clara driving . . .
And so, when she leaves the party suddenly, you
follow, and find her in tears, having at last
placed a call to her parents (missionaries, Baptist).
What do you say? You say, "My first love got married
today," if you're drunk enough.

Late Words to C.

How strange, and like you, not to write me
when you saw my poem, but to send
your picture with the baby
to your cousin the writer, Anne's friend, oddly sure

(or not caring?) that it reach me . . .
What resembled you most was your embroidery,
the big threads
tacking over such terrain to the simple flower.

It was everything of yours I've ever seen—
corny, but unconfidently corny,
and so full of longing as the sea . . .
as when I heaped you with unsolid yearnings:

the good die first and the earth takes the long ship
far into itself under the very first
breaking of lilacs; life is the thunderhead
heaping and heaping over the level towns

and courthouses, to the small
city eyes on the buck-tan seat-cover;
overwhelming our wills . . . One day your first
boy ran his car at you on the dusty road

where you walked out with another,
then crashed to miss a rabbit . . . When you told me,
I knew you were my wayward soul outside me
that wouldn't understand me . . .

But no: you were hoarding, hiding

for the good, unconfident life; you took it always
beyond me up, wild and bewildered, in your words,
in your unclasping fish-shaped ring;

                        and stood free,
elusively solid: your grandmother's house; your child.

II

It's May and we're walking: early
heat-wave, blowzy forsythia . . . "Think:
it's two years from now, Alan, we're juniors;
we're very grown-up now, we laugh

to think how seriously we took all this . . ."
I say I don't want that, I want
the truth of my passion; but can't
try to touch you, awed

by the width
of your milky throat, the column
of your more powerful speech (I later
learned that you always wished smaller) . . .

And the year opens behind you: the acrid wash
of fruit-depth in the leaf, and the cross
the dry winds make in the empty heaven,
carrying dust past a thousand cities,

and I'm still back home, writing to you, dust on the moonish
untraveled plains of my face . . .
I wanted my life to stop with you; then stopped
more than I wanted, an early-chilled scholar;

and could not wish to recover
anything, when we met again in Cambridge,
fearing to impose the irony of a present
on the pure, fixed steps of our failure.

You were no longer my fate; and could not,
though we *did* laugh, be less.
But I've been to New Bedford, where my only novel
lingers unwritten, your unseen companion,

and saw nothing but August heat,
a detour, warehouses in a neighborhood
incongruously lapsed to fields; a low white
bridge, and the bay was passed;

and so I knew I had grown without you,
without that first, piercing brilliance of awakening
where I had thought life centered; unless it is
the point where you are missing.

                             Here on in,
nothing resembles you but your embroidery.

Bernini's Proserpine

It was the first time a really sumptuous girl had taken his hand,
and Rome lay before them: the Spanish

Steps' Cinderella night-piece, dream-whitecaps
falling/rising to Bernini's drowning, monstrous boat . . .

They left behind his more glamorous, her more dowdy, friend,
"transvestites like everyone here at this hour,

only which is the boy, do you think?" "Or which is the girl?"
then burst to a run, now close, now arms' length, leaping

three steps at a time, eluding
Americans and more secretive wayfarers,

until they broke at the fountain's inner rim; and stooping
to drink, he saw

through the fine iris of the jet, her hand
furl slightly, a stone shell;

and knew, somehow, that she would hug herself
through the next block, not entirely because

of the catfight in the blackness under a velvety
Rolls Royce, and the one that ran out, its stomach torn . . .

They met the next day for sightseeing, but their talk
had grown distant, though voluble; the other couple

quarreled; and, at last, she stood him up . . .
But they met once more, and because

he was in love, they were somehow
together again; and at the end,

almost as a gift, she told him the story
half-there from the start: how she was picked up,

in Florence, by a distinguished-looking man, who said
he was a millionaire leather-store owner;

was separated from her friend, and then
—not raped, but forced

to do something perverted, at knifepoint,
in a pine wood, faintly lit from an outdoor night club, near Florence.

The man returned her to her hotel, and said that he loved her,
and that he would kill her if she tried to leave.

She left, in any case,
by the earliest train, not asking for help; but was frightened

in crowds; and after—she puts this impersonally—"I couldn't
like the thought of sex, not even a boy holding my hand."

                              *   *   *

And the first time he comes back to Rome, with his fiancée,
she wakes up screaming . . .

"I dreamed you were sitting naked, except for a loincloth,
in a fancy bar; and you said, 'When I was married . . .'

I said, 'You were married? You never told me.'
You raised your martini and smiled, 'Oh yes, in college;

it only lasted a few days. My parents
had it annulled. I was very young.'

I said, 'You never *told* me,' and suddenly
there was broken glass around, and I started to scream . . .''

He shivers, because he *has* never told her; and walking
to the washstand, his hangover dreadful, he mumbles

"Sometimes not even aspirin does much for small
Sienese paintings" (sinus headaches)

not even in—his first letter home—"a city
where one is never out of the sound of water."

II

That the oldest city grew
                    around that moment's knowledge
(never exactly known, a hundred times imagined):
                                the centuries' breath
gone out in a single night from the pockmarked stone,
at the unknown hour when the water
                        is dead in the deep tanks,
in the mouths of men
                    with the mouths of snakes and birds speaking
out the backs of their skulls . . .

                    After their last meeting, all night
when he tries to doze, touches pour
                    over the stone Proserpine of her body;

3 4

he sees himself draw a sword, and plunge it
                              into the soft underbelly of Death;
and at last, when he knows he will not sleep,
                                                  his bones
rise light as to Judgment, confessing
                    their wish to dance naked with the shattered husks
of arches . . .

                                        Morning comes
as if it were an endless plain, with laundresses
                              on the roof of it, singing
like Tosca's shepherd, some
unplaceable

                        Io de' sospiri

That the city lives around you
gone
            with your long stride, coarse tongue, and Holly-
                                                  wood eyes,
thrilled in the *son et lumière*
when they turned the Forum pink with Caesar's blood,
and really mad at my mocking . . .
                              You were sure
that Fanny Brawne was not good enough for Keats; but likely
to go home to your first lover, a young doctor
who didn't read; you thought a man
was always wrong to let a woman know her power
over him . . .

                  So serious about being
so ordinary, with the sumptuous
assurance of your body: the American
sexualized innocence,
                        demanding, submitting,

demanding to submit
with innocent right to the thousand strengths and prices
of men, harsh and lavish *Fortuna*

                   —the World
come with flowing, tanned stride to the city that is
the World!

                but with the ghost
of a pursuer . . .

I have imagined him as a stone, fixed in place
in a city whose only flowers are stones,
through which the heat comes and goes fiercely, on which the light
falls poor and yellow at night

                  for continuous wearing;
the sad, dry will of the Medici craftsman against
Fortuna . . .

           as if he wanted to leave in you a language
of stones, of dry heat and wearing,
against that impregnable innocence, adoring
and unable to stand what you were . . .

               for what common rapist
expects a date the next night with his victim?

So that he enters my language, that would have raised you
with it

      in useless love, useless revenge, and the sainthood
of the bones rising . . .

Nothing I knew in you could have prepared you; and yet
you were alone with your story, and told no one;
and ran for the earliest train;

             met me,
tested yourself on me; were shaken,
a little, in your plan for your life; and changed
my dryness with your listening

so that, after ten years, the poem flows never
from my loss, but your weakness and courage

                                 Daphne's laurel
rushing, ramifying space around the
                         penis of the young
scarcely awakened god . . .

a wandering touch in the ages of the city

               as if it were an endless plain, with laundresses
on the roof of it, singing . . .

O fountain mouth, thou giving one, thou mouth.

III

A Progress of the Soul

In the beginning there are your limbs crossing simply
as the beams cross in the summer cottage ceiling
—pine-soap smell from the bath—

and there is a story, that goes as many ways
as the cobwebs in the corner. In it, the dead get married
as often as they get baptized in Brigham Young's
Temple, and through the same medium, our pale bodies.
Before you have pubic hair you see the gown
Grandmaman is willing to your bride; you must cherish forever
an invitation to your mother's wedding . . .
O the legions of names that will never have faces, the cancers
that grew on them, as if they were the faces . . .
And the young sit uneasily, stiffly as wood, at the point
that the threads all somehow insist on coming back to.

But the young have intangible allies: the senses
waiting to blossom like deep horns into the skull
and open the echoing valleys; so the outside
arrives in a thunderous surf. One day a lilac
sprig sways, and you are shaken from head to foot with the vertigo
of *why here and now go on at all,* when you blink your eyes.
Then the bad old story is over, and the poem
begins, that goes nowhere, but only deepens and glows.

> Have you felt this? the school rocked
> to the roots, the floors weird planes and sliding—
> the gulf of the future
> that hides in bones, turning
> all first loves' faces to statuary . . .

the love of the thought of your thought made
of green cells . . .

But how sluggish the blaze looks to those who are still in the story!
The boy who slouches, one leg tossed high over
the chair-arm, and answers with hateful over-politeness,
his mind on negligees far as foam on the beaches of China,
seems hardly alive . . . As they try, so they think, to reach him
with their barbed remarks; as they go on trying, his anger
fogs their lives with the deathliness they see in his.
O the endless summer coastal fog
of the photo they live in! the Fourth-of-July lights worming
the cataracts of my blind grandmother's eyes!

So that, years later, the flashes
catch at you oddly: was it really your great-
grandmother who died dragged
by a riding horse through the Bois de Boulogne?
and her husband, the gentle
composer, Ferdinand de Croze, who pined
away and died within a year
after leading Grandmaman
through the ice caves up Monte Rosa?

And then you know you will live in a bare white room,
its splendors books and the covers of books, and tiptoe
against all that entangles you back and smaller—the musty
taste of cabbage, small flocks
listed in the chinks of the nomad rug—unless
you can imagine what is nowhere now, can make
the black dots of the photo flush with dots of rose.

For My Grandfather

F. A. Bächer, 1874–1968

We were putting our shears away after trimming cypress
at the end of August, when the coast goes clear and dry
to the level light,
when I tried to convince him by the medieval proofs:
that nothing happens without a cause, and so
the causes must rest somewhere, in God . . .
He wouldn't stop asking, "But what causes God?" And then,
still chuckling, but moved, "No, the universe
goes on forever, but we have finite minds;
our minds aren't made so as to understand that . . ."

I resisted the infidel, that goes
without saying; but something started
in spite of me, at the dignity of his thought:
how he set his own mind
      beside itself,
as a useful tool, to increase immensity;
as he laid his garden gloves near him, on the stone wall—
each crinkle
    ridged in the even, magnifying light from which
the evening star would, in an hour, sharpen—

and set himself down beside them, saying "Oop-a-la."

43

Frizzled John Dryden

---

der du, mein Vater, seit du tot bist, oft
in meiner Hoffnung innen in mir Angst hast . . .

RILKE

Frizzled John Dryden with a narwhal's horn
(The one true unicorn), from whose rare air
My father came with a silver two-day beard
Down to chafe, like Moses,
At childish things: my lists of child-kings
And martyrs, toy torture-engines for my teachers . . .
Old lithograph, old father
Standing me now and ever
In good stead,
Where shall my roots clutch in your paper ground?

I loved the fragile books, their cooling touch
That shelved me tightly up in my small bed;
For it was there
In the cool of the day, when the courtyard rang, a tiger
Would stalk me down the pathway to the bathroom:
Rage, the birth of song.
Did it bring emptiness or peace, those long
Saturday afternoons when the winter shadowline
Crept up the buildings, while the radio blazed
Tannhäuser, that my father hated? I too sang
The dream in the siren's grotto, and came back,
The staff the Pope would not bless white with flowers.

Where was the one true song? Old lithograph,
Dead father,
What masks of the tiger-Christ, what holy bodies
In the easy mind, began in your renunciations:
These words you are forever freed from reading . . .
All lay in my hands, mere brilliance.
I fear to see my mind
Extend itself through time,
Sharpened and shined; I fear

Hamlet at rest, the ice-
Blue blade crooked like a pencil
In the etched, ghostly hand.

Trois Gymnopédies

for my father, George Williamson, 1898–1968

My father requested that "Trois Gymnopédies" by Erik Satie be the only music played at his funeral. The italicized couplets in *Dark Ages* comes from a fictional morris-dance in the mystery novel *Death of a Fool*, by Ngaio Marsh; other thefts are from Huizinga, Donne, and my father's essay "The Libertine Donne."

THE PACIFIC GROVE GRAVEYARD

If the Judgment never comes to alter
your quarrels, Father, possibly the foghorn
will do as well, deep-thrumming
through the two hundred yards
of sand to your grave.
Like a severer violin,
I would say, if you had liked them.

Once you taught me to know
its voice from the quarrel-
voices of old seals
rounding under my sleep.

Now the shy deer come and crop
the memorial chrysanthemums
clean to the wrists of stems.
                         How often
you tiptoed over the floors
of the house you designed with your own
hands, and that never stopped booming,
to howl at them,
                    as they nibbled
frail "natives" in the moonlight fog.

When I think of you I think
of the outmoded ages: the Iron Crown
of the Lombards; processions and
bells; the slow and exact punishments,
the barbarous, tearful reunions;
                                    and especially
what Huizinga mentions, the absolute
separation of day from night.

      It is not just that I stood
before the small gate to Duke Humphrey's library,
and saw the cloudy, waxy leather rise
to the heraldic rooftree,
your heaven, gained
by your shy illuminator's awe, that I
stand outside, barred
by the cruder presumptions that have made me, me.

As from before a great fire
your face emerges, dancing
      in its old shame,
driving your Aunt Amanda
to church behind the thousand-farting drayhorse;
red, bulbous, elf-light, Swedish,
the rawest
and finest face I have yet seen on this earth,

Mr. Peanut and the old dill pickle,
and little Eheu,
and "Think, think, thou wast made in a sink"
as you scurried, half-naked, into the warm kitchen . . .

      Once for a looker and all must agree
      If I bashes the looking glass so I'll go free

But your face darkens like a mountainside,
"Honor thy father and mother,"
and wanders off all day to read
in wounded, important displeasure.

And I and my friends appear, chanting
the names of our devils: Shit
   the First, Fuck the First,
   Mannerhater the Great,
and dream of the island where we are four kings
and the parents are kept in dungeons.

I see the long gray country rope you once
lashed me with,
for shaking it at you
when you called me a crybaby.

Then, nothing . . . rain-light . . . sad breath
as though still climbing the long stairs
of Chicago . . .
                One winter in Kansas
you were measured for a Christmas overcoat
and thought it was for your coffin.
On the last day, you wished to be taken from the hospital
and thrown by the side of the road.

   Here comes the rappers to send me to bed
   They'll rapper my head off and then I'll be dead

But I can never get
around the crooked corners of your smile.

Choosing the coffin,
unfinished redwood,
                              searching
the plasterboard record-stores of Monterey
for the one music, Erik
Satie's *Trois Gymnopédies,*
                              telling
the distinguished guests to stay away;
                              leaving my father,

where he taught me to know
a landscape not to the heart's liking,
no image of its peace, but cypress
tightened to the shape of wind
                              but you loved it, singing
"My little gray home in the West," as you pulled down the driveway.

                    *   *   *

In the year of the Crash, when Hart Crane
fought his parents for the strength of an instant's writing,
you gave half your salary to yours,
gave up your poetry,
and waited (fifteen years)
                              to have a child.

But set out gaily to be death on feeling
unfused with intellect
                              off to gay/gray London,
you and Mama schemed to give each other
a first edition of Lord Rochester,
long watched, with anxious pricing, in its window
                              shadowed by the British Museum.

Were your twenties lighter-spirited than mine?

In your essay I at last sit reading,
you three years dead,
you argue that John Donne
"may not have violated his own integrity"
if, on "plumbing the emotional depth of that
inconstancy" that first so pleased him

> So flowes her face, and thine eyes, neither now
> That Saint, nor Pilgrime

—an invisible darkening, a moon eclipsed, reason's pale taper
more windblown—
                    he turned to the single Light.

After one operation, you went back
to Camp-Meeting terrors: Hell
a great ring of heat pressing you down,
                                        afraid
it might graze the hems of those who stood by
robed in mysterious coolness.

But you died the modern way, knowing
the strength of your disease, but not its name,
with no preachers or Bibles, but your peculiar God,
and the tiny bright-horned marble bull I brought you
from Crete, I don't know why . . .
                              You angered Mama
by your habit of only sleeping sideways,
your hand closed on the bed's steel guard-rail;
you apologized, saying
"I've spent so many nights in hospitals
I began to feel it was friendly."

And later, open-armed
for the last cardiogram,
ringed with wife, son, an outer sphere of nurses,
you said, "My faithful people,"
your eyes dark violets
like a farm boy's the first
time he thinks a girl likes him.

Carmel, September 1968/Charlottesville, December 1971

Hyde Park at Thirty-Five

What only crept up on you while someone lived there
becomes the city: the blocks empty with greenness
from 29th Street south; only at the corners, one

apartment house, with its deep courtyard, bull's-blood
brick and thorned lanterns, stands—as Englewood
Station, where you last saw your father whole,

stands crisped exact by fire, as on the Day,
with one lone watchman waving the trains through . . .
And, of course, what is incorrigibly the new

persists: the quonset Neighborhood Club from childhood,
brown blockhouses for the old . . . So it's with
a kind of falling asleep, a hush and curtain,

unhesitating, your block begins its scale
of ivory, orange, black, and red-and-black
and wine-red brick. The concrete shield-shaped medallions,

the checkerboard tile . . . And now somewhere a real
piano, with that untuneable summer thinness,
staccato note by note, begins to arc

Scarlatti across the world. It sends you round
the block, restless as cottonwood, to what
you once passed eyes downcast, the still, backset houses

of Laura, Karen—tentative dry reachings
for the freeing name—to find
you look straight through to glass, a Gothic, vined

back window. And in that weightlessness, you think
again of your father: how he came here late
and many times uprooted; how this address for him

was accidental, sad, a place to write immobile
(as you do now) between his bed and a slice of winter
sunlight past smokestacks—that, for you, is ruby-solid,

except the music, the reaching . . . You return, and penetrate
the back court far enough to see his window,
then melt like a ghost as the janitor's son, the janitor

now, his father's great-bellied image, turns
from the new steel fence at the alley-entrance. Turning
at the corner, you vow, *when I can feel I stand*

on solid ground, I'll bring my daughter here;
yet know the words form happily because
supererogation, not that first glimpse when

it, the medallions blazoned above your windows,
all totters, hangs; and then—*O grave where is*
thy victory—goes, like a dream's glassy shadows,

into the farthest waters that you are.

Good Dreams Are Shown
in Nightmare Theaters

I

"Do you ever dream about heaven? I used to,
when I was little."
"What was it like?" "Oh, many beautiful rooms . . ."
The child tries to imagine that, pushing a heavy door
to a vague fall of light from a gray cupola,
and the people remote, far off down the polished floor . . .

"All dreams are shown in Nightmare Theaters,"
he announces one day,
"even good ones. Because you buy your ticket first,
and you don't know it won't be a nightmare, till it ends."
When she says, "But darling, good dreams aren't nightmares,"
he reminds her
of the prettiest dream she had, when she was small:
how there was a Swiss village on the ledge
above her bedroom window—houses, shops, and people
cuckoo-clock size
walking in and out all day, shopping and talking . . .
She cried and cried, when she woke and it wasn't there;
and wouldn't get out of bed
until Grandpapa promised to draw it, and pin it there.

"So?" she asks impatiently. "So, that dream
was shown in a Nightmare Theater." "No, no"—she cries,
her voice wounded and catching—"that was a *good* dream!"
"That's right," he says in triumph:
"Good dreams are shown in Nightmare Theaters."

Stories threaded through places: Daddy's University
with its glassed-in
corridors between courtyards, little bridges, bells;
Snow White the playground behind my nursery school,
flinty in autumn, gloomy under solaria,
where the boy rode by on his bicycle one day
and you asked me to guess his age. We agreed he was ten.
"Will I be ten someday?" You said, "I don't know.
I mean, *really* you will; but one can't know."

And Psyche, left at the hill's prow
(beside the sunken garden), where a breeze
lifted her with your voice to gorges-high,
window-high rooms
she wandered alone, the unseen husband answering
perfectly, until the sisters
whispered, *a monster was promised,* and she raised
the lamp, to grasp . . .
           And then the labors, perfectly
executed, but endless, grain from chaff from grain,
for the envy of Venus . . .
             That May afternoon
grew so suddenly long, learning how imagination
puts spaces inside time, palace rooms
gold traps the spirit wanders, losing count
love from hate from love—

             the story I later
saw twine, around clocks in houses like your mother's,
its twins with butterfly wings.

III

It is not easy to be the child of Great Lovers,
when one is also a replacement for a dead child.
As I grow older, I find your perpetual
candelabra glitter on things
easier to understand and harder to numb out . . .

You begin their story, a hundredth time, for my friends:

"Mother was a pupil of Camille Saint-Saëns.
But she could never go back to Europe. Father was Dutch,
of course, and merely well-off. He met Mother
on the cruise she was sent on to recover
after her mother was dragged to death by a horse
in the Bois de Boulogne. Oh yes—"
                                        your voice
dances on, across a few momentary
gasps—
            "and *he* died, too,
her father, Ferdinand,
they said, of a broken heart—but that's all nonsense,
because the heart doesn't break . . ."

(And Peter, all Tennessee gallantry, saying lovably,
"Of course it does! It does!")

                              "He was the Liberal
black sheep of the family. If he had lived, and met Father,
there might not have been an elopement. But, those aunts!"

After the Restoration, they understandably
didn't want to meet the *polloi* who'd killed their cousins,
so they made their gardens open on each other's gardens,

5 6

and left their great block—all embassies now, rue
de Grenelle—once a year, uncomfortably, to use
their permanent boxes at the Opéra.

On the *14 juillet,* they painted false
black windows on the street-side, so that fewer
of the stones the people threw would break the real ones.

Because the heart doesn't break . . .

Coming out of the ormolu into the faint
Parisian April sunlight—back for the first time
since your honeymoon at twenty—

                                 "I couldn't

see it when I was younger;
I was too wrapped up in myself—

                           but

what Mother gave up for love!"

IV

And you? Wearing short ringlets,
getting yourself included
on a professors-only cruise
to the Greek Islands; Europe twice a year—
you cannot help enjoying the small play
of your pure choosing; the past loved and diminished . . .

"I could have had a more placid life, with someone different;
but it wouldn't have been *interesting* . . ."

But on the day the doctors
decided it was better not to operate—

We kissed his cold cheek. His lips moved. You said, "He's having
    a dream."
Out on the gravel, you cried a moment,
then said bitterly, "Daddy would be ashamed of me."

You were cool for hours, then would blurt
"George didn't make it" into the telephone; when we were alone,
you ran behind a door to hide the scream
that rose behind you
like the veil of a ball gown suddenly on fire.

You had thought one killed oneself, or else "did *everything*,"
and couldn't stand to see him weigh in less
each morning. His last conscious day, you forced him
forkful by forkful—
                          Psyche
lifting the lamp till the high drop spills and burns—

You fed him until he said "ugh." It was the first
time I ever heard you really apologize.

                          V

If I used to dream
of being taken by surprise to my wedding, too happy, then finding
I'm marrying the wrong person I don't love,
was it your dreams of heaven
turned inside out?

If your slightly complacent worldly sadness
was always something I wished to avoid being,
by optimism, by romantic despair;

if I hoped, in following the wisp of your fragility,
to escape the hard unseen angles of your crystal—

I found the hard edge everywhere,
except in my wife, who wore it on the outside,

and whom I could not help disliking for it, so that
still, at parties, a feather knocks me over . . .

And if Ferdinand, your grandfather, is still
the one relative whose photo I keep showing,
with his Walt Whitman beard and the blurred moon-like object
that lives beside his ear . . .

Still we've been to the far side of Lobos,
where all that still blooms is smoky in midwinter,
equally pleased to notice everything;

we've been to the Basque Hotel,
where, as Anne says, I wouldn't have stuck out
all the French sailors, the colorful swaying queue,
without your intrepidness;

and the instant before our plane back East,
you turn to me
with your self-twisting smile: "You're a kind man."

IV

The Hotel with a View of the Jungfrau

Oh let's be big bears, and roll in the bed of the family
till midnight, reading the detective stories
where grandpa's sweet head turns up in a nightcap of blood,

and pull the fog in tighter around the house,
around the Grand Hotel like a big bronze Alp,
content with the world's guilt, and a slow fire . . .

We read high up in the storm, hearing the glass
peal around us like bells; when we went out,
fifteen trees were down in the *Hohematte,*

and they brought dogs to track through the roots in the air
for something—we couldn't tell, from the German—
but we liked the rain-bearded muzzles, and ate late at the
    Restaurant Schuh.

But we are good children, and always wake up believing
this is where we are purely happy. The air breathes thin;
the long red Swiss rugs lift up at the end, with a sigh.

The patterns are jewel-scale: flowers in the mountain
meadows where we wander all day, sweat and run
till we are happy, then decide it's all right to take pictures.

Knee-deep in goldenrod, trying to hold the good smile,
I hear two British children, invisible as crickets:
"How far shall we go?" "Till we don't want to go any farther."

And we would go there too; but the evening comes back, the mysteries,
the room where you lie, too cozy-red, a curl,
and I tiptoe out, not to hear my own complaining,

and hear it downstairs: the oldest, the family pettiness . . .
the Italian teen-ager, in cowgirl leather, surrounded,
gives me her eyes. And I am, miserably,

her conspirator, not in lust but
understanding. Mountaineering is the only answer.
"We had almost got to the blue knees of the Lady,

half-reclining all day, in her peignoir of ice and air,
when our bodies fell back through the several childhoods,
numbed at long tables, answered one look in four—"

I say, and the *minuterie* goes; skylight; blue stars;
feet liking the fuzz of the old treads, the return.

Mirror-Portrait

for Frank Bidart

There's someone in there, who is still quite free,
but best seen flat-on, not a muscle budging:
virginal, yet always on the brink of loving;
balanced, precipitous, beardless as marble
and almost as clean of the sweat of ancestry.
Taken from sideways, he will clown and fall.
All bones rush too far forwards, and the eye
is his mother's, too aware and sidling; mouth
plumps like his father's, but more febrilely,
down on the click and glitter of a truth.

All good . . . as real people aren't; too good for life.
And yet the eyes *are* serious, musical,
as if—he thinks—they know, if they could tell,
his face out of these violent surfaces.

Customs of the Barbarians

Paolo Uccello's *Saint George*

It is two children, and their pet.
The girl leads by a silk thread; her free hand
lifts, as to say, "how gentle."
The boy is the tin woodman of Oz. He sets
a spear like a pointer into the full eye,
so the blood flows down the fang and tongue of the cry
and settles on the ground, like a thick carpet.

While the tail, chartreuse corkscrew, rips for heaven
beyond the caves of the moon . . .

* * *

Some nights, when he strayed near the door,
he could feel the shape of the cold
killer, mirroring; the hand
reach for the knob, as his . . .

his set the lock.
Then, climbing up on the high white bed, wedged
exactly in the corner of the house,
and brushing her cheek, he thought
of their blood risen to spatter their own walls,
and he wondered what the chairs
did with their long night of useless possession.

He dreamed of missed trains, uncertain plans, long hours
spent holding hands, motionless
with his student, who is a great building of light.
While she went to school to the bearded lady,

and often overslept, perversely wishing
for her bad girlhood back, the room
whose address nobody knew, the dictionary
of an unknown tongue open across her knee . . .

But she cried and cried when he spoke of other women.

Her study door was always closed, his always open,
but they never, never
read a word of each other till the last black comma set.

They knew the star-chart, the bird-book, the wine book, the
       Second Volume
of Julia Child, and the sorrow
of the turtle with the bad eye, stacked in the dime-store tank.

They preferred to make love
in the first afternoon, when the sun, just slipped
into the tallest pine,
cast gold planes they thought their bodies would step onto
out of their clothes.

But they always fought at midnight,
slowly and painstakingly
putting on
the hard heat of the fox, the blue arms of the statue,
voices
ripping the ghost attics,
while the rooms filled
slowly with the ash-crystal of weeping,
and they lay
like broken puzzle-pieces,
like small beasts in the great cave of their bodies,
until morning could find the calm children of the picture . . .

They hung it up, when the bad years were over.

Aubade, Reconstructed in Tranquility

That June, you ritually sent me home to sleep.
When I looked back, only the reed curtains

Waved in your suddenly darkened window. Rows
Of glass lab stairwells loomed down the block toward home.

I liked to compare their night-lights
To timed photographs of the sun rising;

But the real sun crept around to north-northeast,
Where the early freight

Whistled near as a bird-call in the next tree.
Yet the light rose equally, from no direction;

Porch-slats shone like sculpture. I entered
To a single yawp from my pacing cat, and fed her.

Dumb to record all this, dumb to show you
A face not formalized by incomprehensions . . .

Now I towsle your head to wake you in full sunlight,
Yet our days seem to meditate on the hour

That no steps bring me back to, that I can even imagine
Happening to others, and not quite make the connection.

The First Spring Nights

                              Orion down,
the king, the pure rectangle, split
on the green spears of the fir!

and the spring stars coming sparser . . .

White planetrees leap from the night's
thicket   bodiless flames
reminding of bodies,
the first, untouched, and so danced
almost to wind, in the story

and the night still the largest body   lion and virgin
woven near in the soft cloth
of new haze   breath
full of land   so the aerating blood
runs out in despair, crying
for this alone I breathe

so that there is no way to be happy but knowing
one is too far in to measure
as when, in loving, your shoulder
turns to uneven meadow, brightening
with Queen Anne's lace   or your face
small and prim as a doll's
when seen from the other side of the
mountain of my yearning and angry hero.

I touched earth today   I follow
paths of wild onion down my longer arms
and, as I doze off, hum at you
four unconnected notes
the hope of the air

The Mountains

In our first winter here,
                when I was often afraid,
we went there on a weekday
                with my student from Harvard,
hair and surplus-store coat—
                "a Confederate dinosaur."
We saw a wild turkey
                walking the pavement,
deer freezing still in the brush,
                and the little, always white houses
creeping out from Waynesboro
                into the near valleys,
hard winks of sunlight . . .
                How easily one could be killed there,
I thought, *no one would hear*
                yet wanted
still greater solitude, hated
                how each turn to each valley
returned them, never the pure
                blast,
an unpeopled ring of world.
                Yet, somehow,
that came back with me
                wind-burn like red earth under
my cheeks, burning on
                into night: a statue, a target?

And this fall, they're below us
                again, on their road-loop,

square arsenic prefab—

          and I could live there forever:
the danger, the sadness

          of sunlight on linoleum,
the blank family words

          a stillness expanding
like a red shriek/red streak

          up into the hills

A gunshot rings the
ring of mountain folds,
gentling, becoming
a measure of space,
everything nearing the body:
the rattle of dry leaves
on a sapling five yards off
like blocks clapped behind the ear.

And I go one step behind myself   (like watching
from the back seat   as a child
houses thin as old trees   heave up, pull by
one gesture   frozen forever
fixing a tire   a wave from a porch
and the whole life surges through, vertical)
an impersonal sadness   taking my fears
as water resumes a wave
I look out at myself through the rock-
eye of my death.

          Come winter, the trees' bareness
will be a mist, a down   blurring the edges
of the edgeless folding

          low contours
that tell us the mountains are old; show us
the air centuries washing

the summits, palming the watershed
wrinkles, old vase . . .

                    As your friend
sits at the foot of the rock   in a small indentation
fanning her waist-length hair loose to the air . . .
Where you join with her
                    as the talk flows over old
distrust behind unkindness I still resent
Where you do not
                    her sharp and earthier laughter—
                                        love

plays out, flashes back; and we are not divided

as you pull me from behind   with your still look
                    rock-lines and underground pressure
your eyes
                    veins of seawater and ore
loving
                    like someone shaken awake
                    or a blind child seeing with fingers
with your one look
                    that I can hold nothing/nothing holds
                                        against.

Spring Trains

In spring one notices the trains more,
in their unaging childhood:
the rust-red boxcars, the blue-black coal scuttles on wheels,
stopped a long time, then imperceptibly moving
through the new green lash
of the willows . . .

I think they will go by the windows of lonely peaked houses
where someone smudged and beautiful
draws one hair back over the seashell of her ear;
and I think they go to the night I once woke to,
dark peaks swinging from side to side of the sky,
and the rapids beneath shades paler than the snow,
while the Mormon evangelist wheezed in the next chair;
and sometimes I think they go to a secret mountain
in the center of West Virginia,
made of coal so black it is everywhere a mirror,
and you never know the moment of passing through.

Last Autumn in Charlottesville

As we live, the years stretch farther on less feeling,
without linking down to earth,
like the bright-legged spiders that startled us
our first fall here,
building over such immense reaches of air . . .

                                        We grew to wait,

each year, for their webs
to catch our eye, out of the first clarifying tingle
of morning cold—like crystal-lines in the air.

Will we dream of them, when we leave here?
Or what will fill this space?
Something must tell us
we have lived six years, not handed everything
to the delirium-of-the-depths of time.

Perhaps I will remember the clean pinyness
of the house, when it was still all there to furnish,
even the night-echoes too sparkling to scare us . . .

Or how we stayed a few days into Christmas vacation,
with downtown almost silent, dwarfed
under its radio tower,
and came home one night to find
not a light on in our whole neighborhood;
how we hesitated on the doorstep, watching our trees
throwing their black points
around the strangely lightened and pearly sky.

Childless Couple

Now the spaces open to them:
one friend instantly dead; one gone in misunderstanding
and resentments . . .
There are none to replace them;
and the girl students' faces are no longer glass.
It's like something—wheels—reversing; it's
the far side of the moon.

He thinks: *I've never taught better, been more instantly*
sure of myself, when I write;
and there's no lie in that.

She talks of a garden; they talk, too much, of their money.

When they walk
together, they settle themselves in all the houses
that have odd nooks, oval stair-windows,
or pointy, unexpected further floors.
Houses deep as money, as long gardens,
as the grandfather stillness of the wavy glass . . .

And the children's things
bracketed in the high dark, busy and stagy . . .
Once he saw the child's hat hung on the wall, like a picture.
How much is done to make us believe the world wants us,
when only we could
think of wanting, not just things, but a world!

They were animals every year, but not until this one
small British bears, well-behaved, with insides possibly
excelsior: Wuff and Padd.
As if growing heavy and woolly would call something
from beyond the sky to feel welcome, give them their names . . .

What? They don't know, any more; and the winter is ending.

And the dead friend, and the friend grown hostile,
tiptoe back down the years, removing
things small and unnoticeable, as if the firelight
paled, a minute, on all those tight-drawn circles . . .

"Did it really, Wuff?" "No, Padd . . ."

And the spaces open to them, the music
of the far side, that nothing
will catch back into any circle;
that is oneself continuing, only sifted
a little eerily higher
passing the equal stars.

Heaven

Cottonwood: boats of white thread
going, it seems, nowhere,
carrying a seed invisible
as the soul of Pharaoh, among the little servants . . .

I remember how, in such a week
dividing spring from summer
—a desert leatheriness on the June leaves—
coming home from church, I tried to imagine heaven

and got as far as a sense of pattern
before and after life,
its stained glass slightly tilted
to the summer air:

the old waiting for completion as the young
wait to know of the flesh;
somewhere, at each moment, an eye of breaking vessels
meets an eye that does not hold a single name.

Things the houses talk of,
with their smooth lintels, their unblinking eyes.
The spaces between the stars
that contain us, though none of us will ever go there.
The ephemerids holding it all in their one day.

And then, this was lost; for years I thought of time
as a series of lonely, brightly-lit rooms,
each a little different,
but with no ladders up or down into
layers of other life . . .

But the first time we wrongly thought that you were pregnant,
I heard a voice in a dream
saying, "We are going to the power station";
and I looked down, ecstatic, from a mountaintop,
at a russet brick building, grilled but windowless,
smokestacks rising among great elms;

and then I dreamed we were on a train, all windows,
heading into the lights of a coastal city,
and someone said, "You will be on this train forever."

I woke up feeling that I had been in heaven.

Presence

---

for Peter Taylor

The sad, because unspeaking, smiles
overbrimming
among too many people known too slightly
but halfway loved,
in large rooms where the light shades and flickers
on the untended gardens, vines and harpstrings,
of the old wallpaper . . .

Whom do we speak to when we speak on these
stages we make of our lives?

My friend, a week before his heart attack, showing us
a house bought to recall how Tennessee
recalled Versailles—the rooms
too square, too large, but only two to a floor,
the ratio
of a city apartment to a child's eye . . .

What set you writing your best in years there? Your portrait
done by a girlfriend, at nineteen,
across your desk each morning, trustworthy
in the simple way it had not come to focus,
but with an immortal's
electric-blue hair?
                    "—oh, painted beautifully,
sang like an angel"—your voice pure 19th Century
and eyebrow lewdly raised . . .

"My brother wanted to be like me in everything,
but I only watched the effect I made on girls.
I loved my mother so,
if she had cared for me, it might have ruined me—
but she only cared for parties, the Great World."

While your friends' children, feverishly, kept bringing sticks
from the wood's edge, and laid them
in the simplest structure that rises—
a mounting triangle, threes on threes on threes . . .

Or that Andes plane crash: "But Jane, would you eat Alan?"

Jane swung
a light fist at you for that, out on the porch;
and then we left you
in the shadow-netting of a country summer,
weak light, wide leaves, wide wings . . .

Will we go into death as into sleep
on that close night? Or do we really live
in fragments of what we thought came only in dying?—
the Dream a ratio of spaces receding
and the faces going wide in them, blurred yet stilled,
as if the initial peopling of our lives
ran in reverse,
until there is only the ratio, and first
hinting-through of color
to hold—but hold to the end.

Old Toys Come Back

for my daughter Elizabeth

As from before the ages they come forth,
wholly forgotten, wholly pleasing; stripped
of detail, as if meant for flight—this white wool "dog,"

homemade, smooth as a lancing seal, and awkwardly
arrow-like, on its four back-slanting legs;
these folk-art lambs on blue . . . Once here, they nag us

with what they have left behind them; say that soon
The New House in the Forest will come, its thin frame rising
in a clean stand of trees; and *Scuffy the Tugboat*

will slip the hand and come down, past falls and sawmills,
with the man in the polka-dot tie to reach and catch him
as he passes the tip of the farthest breakwater . . .

So you have come down, scarcely smiling yet, liable
always to doze off, with motion and the outdoors;
stranger than a log . . . How shall we know to love you,

if not instructed by what loved us before
we knew our face or name?—messengers at
the landfalls of presence, shape; with the washed smoothness

the Platonists say the chairs will have, in heaven.

A NOTE ABOUT THE AUTHOR

Alan Williamson was born in Chicago in 1944. He studied at
Haverford and Harvard. His poems have appeared over the past
twelve years in *Poetry, The New Yorker, Partisan Review,
Ploughshares,* and many other magazines. He is also the author
of *Pity the Monsters: The Political Vision of Robert Lowell.* He
has taught at the University of Virginia, Harvard, and Brandeis
and now teaches at the University of California at Davis. He is
married and has one daughter.

A NOTE ON THE TYPE

The text of this book was set on the Linotype in a type face
called Baskerville. The face is a facsimile reproduction of types
cast from molds made for John Baskerville (1706–75) from his
designs. The punches for the revived Linotype Baskerville were
cut under the supervision of the English printer George W.
Jones. John Baskerville's original face was one of the forerunners
of the type style known as "modern face" to printers—a "modern"
of the period A.D. 1800.

Composed by Maryland Linotype Composition Company,
Baltimore, Maryland.
Printed and bound by American Book – Stratford Press,
Saddle Brook, New Jersey.

Designed by Judith Henry.